I'LL WRITE YOU A PRESCRIPTION TO LOVE

Adrian D. Weaver

Cover designed by Tammie T. Polk

Printed in the United States of America

First Printing: July 2020
Amazon/KDP

ISBN-13 **9781735439402**

CONTENTS

VOLUME I

CHRISTMAS NIGHT

A mysterious moon, a winter's night
Snow falling down in a wonderous sight

Hand in hand as love is so near
Loving you more as the snow glows clear

We walk in the snow with it's white diamond shine
I look in your eyes and knew you were mine

I held you to my heart so close and so near
Wiping from your face a snow drop tear

I kiss your lips covered with shiny snow flakes
So cold from the snow by taste so great

We fell to the snow in the dusty white trail
Snow failing on your face made like a crystal white
vail

We close our eyes and kiss for a while
Our bodies and love had travel the mile

We open our eyes and looked around
A hickory smoke, a oak tree brown

A log cabin I said that was sturdy and strong
This our moment which nothing can go wrong

On that Christmas night so cuddle and snug
Lying together on a bear skin rug

This holy night, we made love
While a fiery star shined from above

I wish this beautiful night would never end
For I'll always be your lover and special friend

This romance we had we'll always remember
And that snowy night on the 25 day of December

FROM HERE TO ETERNITY

I've stood in under stormy nights
While the moon glows with a heavenly light
And thought of the day we were dress in an elegant
white

I look in your eyes as you walk down the aisle
With that lovely expression and beautiful smile

And through the windows, there came the sun
With a loud ring, the church bells rung

I took your hand as you stood before me
Then I said I'll always love thee

The presence of the lord was very near
And from your eyes drop a lonely tear

The vows we spoke were from our souls
That reflects our lives and our future role

The ring I said, as I held your hand
And slip your finger, the beautiful wedding band

Then we said Baby "I do"
The people look at us
And knew the love would be true

I kiss my bride, as tears of joy came from the people
While church bells rung loudly in the high steeple

We walk down the aisle hand in hand
With you as my woman, and me as your man

I came through in my sudden daze
As my eyes were watery and in a shiny glaze

It started to rain as I turned to go home
I look as I turn, I was not alone

My wife to be was standing there
While rain falling on us I just look and stared

I took your hand, then I said

Baby, my love, the women for me
Cause I'll always love you from Hence to Eternity

I LOVE YOU

I've dreamed of loving a person like you
To show I care—and to say I love you

The beat of our hearts, could play the rhythm & soul
So here we stand in a loving role

My emotion so strong and also so deep
Yes, I love you for being beautiful and petite

Your heart is as pure as the driven snow
My love and joy I'll always show

A love like you I've always desire
Together our love could is as a golden fire

I could give you rings, diamonds, and gold
But to me that is old

I'd rather give you caring, love, and joy
For I'm a man grown out of a boy

When I think of you leaving—I almost cry
I love you, these words are true, they're no lie

Love is loving and caring
Something hard to explain
Love is also feeling the heartbreak and pain

So I stand the test of time waiting for you
Saying I love you, cause I do!

OCEAN NIGHT

Cold and lonely nights I've thought of you
And how I would prove my love, so true

Our love shines as a ghostly gleam
When were together holding hands on a romantic
scene

I'll look in your eyes under a bright cherry moon
As the light of it shines on the watery lagoon

Your eyes shine as black shiny pearls
As if they were the greatest of three great worlds

The fire of love burns forever more
I'll hold you in my arms and watch the ocean soar

I kiss your lips as we lay down
As the seagull of love make sweet sounds

My hand touches your silk soft skin
As we feel a light breeze, a soft wind

The feelings of love are finally right
Now we make love under the misty dark night

The ocean is our sounds, the waves are our motion
As the air thickens with love and deep emotion

So my angel, I want to be with you
For no other girls in this world could be so true

You're worth more than money, You're worth more
than gold
Til the day I die, you're the one I'll always hold

Expressing my feelings is so hard to do
And also saying J'amoureux

To hold you in my arms is a dream I share
A love like yours is so precious and rare

Three words I speak will be true
Between to great lovers I love you

Holding you in my arms and so romantically evolved
While the joy in our hearts turn and revolved

Damn, I love you, I don't know what else to say
Just that I'll melt your fears and love you more each day

May the fire burn forever, as the ocean flows through
And may our love get stronger as the days come between
me & you

TWENTY-FIVE YEARS OF BLISS

Together we have been for quite a while
Weathering the storm as we travel the mile

Enthralled in each other along the trail
No barriers between us could prevail

The youthful love usurious desire
Yet grow brighter and burn like a golden fire

Fruitful where the times we spent
Interested in the actions as the day went
Vesper prayers uttered for our love to hold
Every year we've spent is more precious than gold

Yes! Our love is beautiful and Petite
Emotions so strong and also so deep
All there is left for one to say
Roses will last and smell so sweet
"Our love will last till death we meet."

VOLUME II

I THOUGHT I'D LOST HER

One night at home, One night alone
I went to the river as the branches moan.

I stood at the bank and gaze at the water
My heart was trouble, and also bother.

Kneeling to the bank, I grasp the sand
It slid through my finger, out my hand.

The sounds from the river, started to rise
Then a ball of water shot into the skies.

The glow of the moon blended with the ball
It stayed in mid-air, it didn't fall.

I looked at the ball, and saw the past
Memories of time that will always last.

The times we walk, we were all alone
The night was so dark and also long.

When I held your hand and help you up
When you bandage my wounds and heal my cut

When I pick you up, off your feet
And rubbed your hair, and put you to sleep

The memories and moments flew threw my mind
All the pleasure & happiness, and cherish times

The flashback of the ball had started to fade
There were tears in my eyes of the memories we made

The ball in the air fell back to the water
As I jumped in and swam, farther and farther

Chasing the memories that I once have had
Splash! Splash! I woke, My face—sad

Until I turn and looked, my dear was there
My love of the memories, the love for which I care

I grasp you, I held you so tight and so bold

Wouldn't let you go, more priceless than gold
I look in your eyes and said from my heart
I shall not leave, I shall not part

As long as I'm with you, I'll always be with you
Til death do we part, <u>I Truly Love You!</u>

MY UNDYING LOVE

I am the man that stands in time
Hoping one day that you'll be mine

Watching the time, as I count the hours
Waiting for that day our love will shower

You were the one that tame my fire
Who lit my emotions and fill my desire?

Their just so much that one can say
Of the joy you bring me every day

I wish time would remain, on one ecstatic scene
Then from my heart, I could tell you what I mean

You are my joy, you are my heart
You are the roots from the trees that won't part

You are the stars, you are the night
You are the person that gives me light

You are the one that I turn to hold
You are the one who ease my soul

But the words I say is just not enough
If I must sacrifice my life, then this is what I must

I hold your hand and give out my love
If I must give up my life, then may Good take me above

I bow to your love and kneel to the floor
To show my appreciation and to say I want more

May you take these words into your heart
And may our feelings stay forever & never part

I truly love you -- always

THE LAST NIGHT WE WERE TOGETHER

The last night we were together, we were in the park
And holding on to each other, in the moonlit dark

It's hard to think, we will be apart
My heart will be close, I will be far

And then I look, into those eyes
A tear that fell, glistening with the moonlit skies

The tear rolled down, until it touch my face
And made a path, with an unsteady pace

What was I to do, for a girl so true
No words could fit, not even I love you

I look at the moon, and said a prayer
The moon glowed, with a holy glare

There in the lake, that was calm and blue
With ripples of waves that the wind blew

And from the water, was lifted a rose
That was red as a heart with petals that glowed

A strong wind came by, and blew the rose to our feet
With a fragrance so rare, and with a smell that's so sweet

I picked up the rose, and handed it to you
You look in my eyes, there was nothing I could do

The sadness and pain, I truly could feel
As water in my eyes, had started to build

A tear fell, on and off my face
Another and another, as my heart started to race

And then you spoke, and said these words
As long as we're alive, the rose want die
The rose stand for love, so please don't cry

So I lifted your chin, and kiss you lips
With precious passion, but my heart was ripped

Tears in my eyes, I said this to you
With pain in my heart, these words I construe

This may be, our last night together
But the love we share, will last forever and ever
I Love You!

OUR CHRISTMAS NIGHT

One cold and windy, winter's day
Thick snow, icicle, and clouds of gray

My flame, my angel, the joy of my life
My one to hold, through all the cold nights

I plan to make this a joyous time
For a woman, a friend, who's been so kind

This Christmas night, I've fix for you
Our first together, I'm saying I love you

I took your hand, lead you to our tree
Lights so bright, bulbs so shiny

I turn to your face, stared into your eyes
So stary, shiny, they were stars in the skies

The glow from the tree, lit up the room
Then out of the blue, played a mellow toon

The moment, the passion, was perfect and right
For once we had peace and happiness, in our life

I extend my arms, I held you tight
Not wanting to let go, not this night

Cause this is the night, that we belong
For this is the night we have long

The present I give is from me to you
The present is love, the present is true

As I held you in my arms, we look at the tree
The star at the top, glisten with glee

But the star that was real, the star in the night
The star that glisten, the star that was bright

It shined on us, which brought us a cheer
From the look in our eyes, we were sincere

I kiss your lips, as our hand would meet
The kiss was forever, gentle and sweet

We confessed our love, once again
Made love all night, which did not end

This night of Christmas, was truly for love
The star that shined, shined for our love

The year is ending, but my love will not
Forever, Forever, my love want stop
Merry Christmas

WE PROMISED FOREVER

It was a dreary wet night, while I was at home
With no one to hold, and me all alone

So I walk to my chair, and took me a seat
As the rumble of thunder, put me to sleep

I dreamed of a promise, that I thought would come true
Forever together, just me and you

This dream was so different, but yet so real
Every touch and every emotion, I truly could feel

The love in my heart, had entered my mind
With a touch of joy, that also shined

I found myself, by a tree

With a bridge in front, on a brook from the sea
A dim light was shining, as I look around
I followed the light; a house is what I found

I went to the window, and saw a bright light
Which came from the fireplace, a fiery sight

The wind came by, blew open the door
A lady, a beautiful lady was on the floor

I walked towards the lady, so soft and warm
But in the fireplace, a ball had form

It shot out the room, faster than light
Off it went, deep into the night

I ease to the floor, gently with grace
I grabbed her hand, and kissed her beloved face

Her eyes had open, and looked into mine
As the love we saw, had started to shine

She touch my cheek, and then I awoke
The dream I was in, was suddenly broke

I arose to the lady, in that beautiful dream

Who was lying on the floor, of that romantic scene?
So, we took a walk down the lonely pass
Finally, we were together, alone at last

And from the ground, a flower I took
As we came across, the bridge and the brook

We stood on the bridge, and watch the sky
We stared and looked; the ball of fire flew so high

It flew by us, and into the brook
Splash in the water, with a picture it took

It was filled with love, happiness, and joy
And one little girl, and one baby boy

The promise we made, was becoming true
I thank the Lord, for me and you

WE WISH ON A STAR

Star shine so bright, in the misty dark night
Holding hands, under the angelic moonlight

Looking in your eyes, while a breeze passes through
And whispering to your face, I need you

A deep emotional kiss, so hard to resist
While we cling together, in the rain wet mist

Holding you in my arms, as your heart beats near
And wiping your raindrop tear, as I crest your fear

I look in your eyes, as a star started to fall
As the moment of love, begin to call

The vows I've made, are all true
Which came from my heart, and were promise to you

Blood moon set, we were engaged
Bounded forever, till the end of our age

You I've chosen, out of all the rest
And see if our love, can with stand the test

Now we must fight, to stay together
And see if our love, can with stand the weather

May the passion of love, hold us forever
The Love we hall, will last forever and ever!!!
Always & Forever

YOU WILL BE MINE

My days are sad, my nights are long
Missing my family, and wishing I was at home

My heart is hurting, & crying with tears
Missing the hugs, that swept my fears

I pray to God, to give us swept
But sometimes I figure, we must do this ourselves

Seeing the memories, that go through my mind
Day after day, time after time

The memories of holding, within my arms
Protecting you all, from all harm

Looking out the window, at the glowing moon
Making a wish, that I'll be home soon

Seeing you in person, brighten my heart
And makes me forget, how long we've been apart

I'll always love you no matter where you are
I'll always love you no matter how far

All I can do, is look at the dream
That we will be one & love will be our theme

It helps my heart, and awful lot
But still in my heart, there is one lonely spot

Will that day come, will it be
Will we get married, you & me

Oh! How I cherish the thought, of me & you together
And after that day, love gets better and better

We've waited to long, to give up this day
With God as our guide, we'll find a way

As time goes own, our fears will go
As we show everyone, that love is our miracle

As I said before, now it means more
Lady, my love, you made me sore

One more mountain left to climb
And after that day, you will be mine!

VOLUME III

HOW MUCH I MISS YOU

I sit at the window, watching the rain
Pat! Pat! Counting the raindrops, feeling the pain

A pain that's gentle, I also can feel
A pain that shows me, that this love is real

So much to say, but nothing I can do
This far away, I say I love you

I look at this rain, falling & falling
Wish'in I could hold you, I keep calling & calling

I see you down a pathway, so far but so close
Hoping & praying, what I see is not a ghost

I ran & I ran, chasing for your love
The more I ran, harder the rain poured from above

I ran til I fell, then you started to fade
I called for your name, all I saw was dark shade

Tears from my eyes, Oh! How they poured
Saying to myself, O Help Me! Help me Oh Lord!

The rain drops & tears, were from me missing you
I never got the chance to say I Love you

My love, my love, calling you in my sleep
I felt a present, I wake & heard a calm weep

You were there! This was for real
I fell to my knees, crying with chills

You picked me up & held me in your arms
I felt so protected, you were just so warm

I held on to you, for the remainder of the night
Not wanting to let go, this felt so right

This is how I'll feel, until I've died
And even then, I'll be by your side

Hold me again so I can hold you
Did I ever tell you I Love You?

I'M STILL MISSING YOU

Many days and nights, I've thought of you
So much I want to say, but I'd rather be with you

The love that we have share, has been more than enough
But the days without you, have been so rough

I miss you with my heart, I miss you with my mind
I miss everything include the pleasured times

You warm my heart, by the touch of your hand
Closing my eyes, wishing you were my woman

I've dream so much, nights I was at home
Wishing to God, I would not be alone

Nights I was wishing, you were by my side

Walking and wondering, so we may go hide

We both would sit under the bluish moon
Waiting to feel our love soon

Out lips touch, a kiss so slow
With passion behinded it, the more our love showed

You clinched my body with a bold grip
Then kiss my neck with your soft lips

Oh! I was so happy and fill with joy
That I clinch your body, I wanted more

My eyes were to yours, your lips were to mine
Out bodies were together, this was our time

Slow and gentle, confessing our love
You've taken me away, as if love was a drug

You've been my heart from the time we met
Nothing I've done, I'll never regret

The love that night will last forever
For now I must go
But me stop loving you never

I Love You

JUST OUR LOVE

Who would ever think I would meet someone like you
You know how I feel, you know when I'm blue

The times that we've laugh, & the time we've talk
Each & everyone has been in my many thoughts

Yes I do, I do love you
This is true, how much do you

I'm here when you need me, I'm here to the end
As long we're together, I'll be more than a friend

Better & Better, after each kiss we kiss
Each minute of a day is a kiss that we miss

I knew this day would come that you & I would be
You & I together, you just for me

We've hugged & hugged, you've held me tight
You made love with passion, such a long night

Making love to you is such a special thing
Like were together, in a sleepless dream

You see how I feel, you see that it's real
Fate is seal, so let's climb this hill

So we are hand in hand, til days are gone
With you & I together, I don't care how long

MY LOVER OR FRIEND

Oh it's been a while, since I've known you
Thank you for being a friend, so true

You came to me, when you heard my cries
And answer my question when there were whys

You've given me happiness, that makes me live
You've been so good, but I have nothing to give

If air was my gift, it would com from my heart
From my heart to your, it's a priceless art

So much has past, in our lives
That if we were lost, you'd be my guide

I'd hold your arm, just to feel safe
Protection from harm, strengthen my faith

I've look for a person to fulfill my life
Someone who cares, and comforts night

You've been right there through thick & thin
I appreciate you for being a damn good friend

Love has been in my face, but I have been blind
No more, I see my love will shine

I'm asking you this, not as a friend
But as a person I'll cherish to the very end

Will you be mine the person I can hold
The deepest passion of love and together grow old

Our love could be like a burning flame
As long as we're together it could not be tame

If you still want to be friends and not go farther
I will not pressure you, I will not try harder

I mean know harm by what I ask
I just wanted something that's meant to last

Your friend or your lover which do you want
Either way I'll still love you

THAT NIGHT

That night was long, and painful to me
Dreams were lost, it seems they would not be

Where will I go, what will I do
My life was basically—wrapped around you

I did not beg that night you left
I loved you that much, I kneeled & wept

But that day is gone, that day is past
These hours & days—do not go fast

They say time does not, which is a lie
Cause if that were true, you would no have me cry

So many smile and many long nights
Beauty & pleasure—so much delight

I've seen you reason, you do look good
I want you back, I wonder if I could

But why should a man, be scared & frighten
His feeling & emotions—he truly is fighting

I guess I'll sit in the night, & cry til I'm tired

And hope that she knows that she is admired

That Christmas night was a painful sight
I shall be thinking her and that night
I still love you!

VOLUME IV

MIDNIGHT AT THE FOUNTAIN

The stars were out, & the moon was full
A summer breeze, very light but cool

A fountain of water, filled with coins of wishes
A flower bed of roses, which are the red riches

The glare from the moon, was shining on us
God was doing this, it was a must

So here I sit, in front of your face
The lady I wanted, I have many times chase

I was confessing my heart, and looking in your eye
You face was blushing, as the butterflies flies

I a rose your chin, as I begin to say
With a deep voice, a stony face

This moment was no different, it was real
From this moment on, our fate was seal

I grab a dozen roses, place them at your feet
Each one stands for a year, that you & I will be

When that twelfth year come, I shall ask you to take a seat
With a diamond in my hand, forever it will be

Your eyes were watery, you place your hand on my face
Soft & gentle, my heart faster & faster, race

The moon was shining, the stars were out
Clearly it was a sign, that's loves about

I will be like a rose & be sweet to you
Just as long as you love me, I'll always love you.

IF IT WAS MEANT TO BE

A day of raining, rain falling down
I stood in a field—I remembered something I found

A young lady that's beautiful, beautiful as the world
Who's heart shines as a water ball would twirled

She was very special, special to me
I stood in this rain, picturing how it would be

But I said to myself, this is a dream
She can not realize how much she means

If she had pain, I would take it off her shoulder
If she was hurt, I would take her hand & console her

While out on the field, I began to walk away

When I caught a glimpse of a flower in a lonely space
The flower was alone not another one in sight
It seems to be crying with tear in the night

I was that flower, that stood on the field
Crying from my heart, living this ordeal

What must I do, not to be like this flower?
Lonely and sad, hour by hour

Why can't she see the goodness in my heart?
The caring, love, & joy that she could be apart

But I shall walk on, with my head up
With God's blessings, I want need luck

Maybe one day, I'll rise & she'll see
Cause if it was meant to be, it will be

YOU CAN NOT KNOW
HOW MUCH I CARE

The night was tired, I began to lay down
My room—still, nothing but silent sounds

My eyes drew heavier, they close shut
A deep sleep near, my pillow I clutch

My mind had wonder, wonder into a dream
To a place my mind had never seen

The place was dark, you could barely see
Their was a dim spot light, it seem to be

I proceeded to walk, not knowing where to go
Just following the light, wondering what it would show

I ran upon a chair, a lady sitting down

She was not happy, her face was filled with frowns

She rose her head & looked in my eyes
Tear after tear, I could feel her cries

I embraced her with compassion & a heart full of love
She was hurting from the inside, she returned the hug

I look in her eyes & wiped that tear
And from me a soft whisper, I'll always be here

She began to hug me, so I picked her up
She kissed my cheek, my heart would touch

We walked away & disappeared in the air
But she cannot know how much I care

CHANGE OVER TO LOVE

A high cliff, and autumn day
Ocean breeze, and a ocean spray

Staring at the water as far as you can see
Holding you close as we lay on this tree

Whispering I love you, I kiss your cheek
You gripped my hand, as I softly speak

The ocean breeze, chills our spine
As we begin to cross this thin line

The sun & the moon, will always change
A repeating cycle that's in our range

From friends to lovers this is what I see
If we cross this line, this future shall be

We stared at the sun, the cycle took place
Our heart beats together, a fast pace race

We laid on this tree as night has fallen
It seemed both our hearts kept calling & calling

I looked in her eyes, I said see what I mean
The change from one, you surely have seen

I must love you a lot, to be out here
To want your heart year after year

I kiss your lips, the moon it shined
The moon was glowing, it must be a sign

Now I know, and yes I do
As long as I'm alive I will love you

God sent this as a message from the above
Two great friend changed over to love

VOLUME V

MY PRECIOUS GIFT

The tree was lit, presents all around
Christmas Eve still, not a sound

Sitting before the tree, thinking of a gift
This is what I want, my spirit it would lift

So, I awoke, with hope in my eyes
Maybe this day he could hear my cries

Would I get the gift or would I not?
Or would I be the person, who just wished a lot

The day has past and night fell
The Lord came through, he will prevail

Holding her hand, I told her this
You are the gift I've many times missed

Our eyes met, so much to be said
No words heard, passion instead

Off we went, into the night
A lot of joy, and much delight

We came across a wishing well
A scent of rose, a beautiful smell

I flipped a coin, in the air
Rub her cheek, as the coin glared

It flew in the air but never came down
No splash no swish, not one sound

Flakes were falling as we kissed
I picked one up, it couldn't be mist

Snow covering us, from head to toe
No origin explained, & why does it glow

She said this is my wish, from me to you
Showing I care, it glows for you

A beautiful gift and snow falling down
What more can I ask for, I have no frowns

Merry Christmas

THE ROSE IS YOU AND YOU ARE THE ROSE

This rose stands, just for you
A vision of joy, covered with droplets of dew

A petal I would place, on your lips
Your emotion I'd touch, your heart I'd tip

This bloom I would place, in your hair
As I kiss--& tell you, how much I care

I'd rub the rose, against your cheek
While dropping petals, at your feet

Spread the roses around the tub
Her feet, gently I rub

Your body I'd dry, with the petals I pick
Every inch of your body, slowly I lick

Quietly you sleep, lying on the bed
I place this rose, beside your head

This one little rose, means a lot
From the end of the stem, to the last tiny dew drop

The flower of love, reminds me of you
And shows you my love, what I will always do

A rose will last as sweet as it smells
Our love will last till all have fell

.

MY SECRET

A spring night, and a pleasant breeze
We're standing in the shadow, of and oak tree

The breeze cool, which tingle the skin
I'm holding you bolding, uplifting divine

I'm feeling my patience, starting to fall
I want to tell my secret, that is all

I look at a star, my eyes are glaze
How do I say I love you, there are so many ways

If I tell her, would it hurt
Should I be quiet, Oh! How does this work

The feeling I have, are no longer the same
I open my mouth to speak, we feel rain

She say to me, it's time to go in
She's walking away, is this how it end

I grabbed her hand, and called her name
Baby, please don't go, please remain

I have something to say, that's from my heart
It's worth more than gold, or priceless art

I must say to you, my love is strong
My feelings are right, but I hope this is not wrong

I picked up a rock, a simple rock
This will last longer than any time clock

A rock is unchanged, through winter or storm
And remains the same, even when it's warm

The rock is my love, this is how it will be
I declare to you, you for me

These two just stood, facing each other
Would they stay friends or become lovers

Til his end, he will always love her
Whether they weren't or whether they were

I Do Love You

MY DREAMING HILL

A blue moon—a cloud every hour
I'm just sitting down, twirling a flower

Clouds I could touch, sitting on this hill
A breeze blowing by, giving a slight chill

The star would twinkle, glimmer & glowed
The dipper above, clearly it showed

My rose I lifted, I smell the scent
I thought of her, my mind—content

The world is precious, but she means more
This lovely woman, I cannot ignore

The trees & the grass, keep us alive
As long as she's with me, I shall strive

We'll ride the clouds, to a romantic place
Walk through garden of roses, at a slow pace

With no sleep I'd walk, to bring her needs
I'd work & work, till my fingers bleed

Some dreams won't come true, some might
Do I have any hope, look at my past life?

The love I hope, is just unreal
But what really counts, is how she feels

While in thought, there was a hurling wind
I stood and said, I miss my friend

A tear of my face, blew into the air
I'm crying, but what do I care

The tear in the wind, hit someones cheek
It's the beautiful lady, I have chase & seek

Adrian are you crying, why do you do so
My feelings I can't hold, they're beginning to show

She gripped my hand, wiped my tear
These scary feelings should disappear

She held me boldly, throughout the night
But would it last, past this night

YOU MEAN JUST
THAT MUCH TO ME

What a lady in elegance, that I have found
She's precious as the earth, and is solid as ground

Beauty you behold, even the one I can't see
That's what in your heart, I wish it to be with me

How did I meet, someone like you?
So rare to the world, did he lead me to you

The lord, was he giving me a gift
My soul she touches, my heart she will lift

I thank him a lot, and give him praise
Cause this lady he sent, could have went other ways

Where would a leaf be without a tree
Without water would there be a sea

And without you, there would be know me

No bulb, no rose, no flower
Without time, there is no hour

That hour—I spend, thinking of you
Counting & counting, tik toks without you

No moon, no night
No sun, no light
No you in sight
No life with new heights

No land to have, there's no earth
No land to grow, there's no dirt
Without you, my heart will not work

You mean to me, the worth of a prayer
The length of your faith, & how much you care

Would I be around, without you?
I'd be a lonely cloud, Far away from you

What I am trying to say, I wish you could see
That you mean, just that much to me

WILL I EVER

Sitting on the steps, I'm just looking off
I remember her touch, it was so soft

But where is it now, it's not around
I can't help, but to keep a solemn frown

She kisses me once, on my cheek
This moment is dear, I shall always keep

Do I miss her, or does she miss me
I know I miss her, this I wonder can she see

Now I sit, & I'm all alone
Her tender touch, has slowly gone

My voice is shaky, & tear are shed
They drop to the ground, as I hold my head

I hide my feelings each day I rise
But they're still there, right by my side

So, I pretend, and even dream
But I find myself asking what does this mean

I stand to my feet, & looked in the sky
Calling out to her, as if she heard my cry

What did I do, where did I go wrong?
But I'm not the only one to sing this same song

I know I've tried, but it seem I've fell
Should I give up, only time will tell

Does she feel like me, I doubt that to be true
No person should feel, this sad or blue

I'm not perfect, nor I'm a saint
But I'll be the best I could be, until the ship sank

I do not deny, her feelings are not for me
I was hoping, just maybe, one day she could see

I extend my hands, as it begins to rain
I rubbed my face to, cover the pain

Will it come true, some say never?
But I'm always thinking, Will I Ever

VOLUME VI

SEEING BLIND

How could one, be so blind
Not to see a heart, that brightly shines

I see her face, almost everyday
Just a few words, is all I had to say

Darkness covered, my eyes for so long
I might be to late, she might be gone

The way I feel, I just walk in the moonlight
I walk past her house, maybe I'll het a sight

One night I walk by, I look at her room
It was a breezy night, a pretty full moon

For a brief moment, I had to stop
I saw her face, my eyes locked

Something happen, from that small time
It was special, something hard to find

I waved to say bye, wanting to run back
If I do, she'll no my heart is attached

Now I walk asking, why I'm blind
Knowing all the time, she could have been mine

But if I had a chance, in the world
She'll mean more to me, than just my girl

I'll love her & lover, with all my heart
And when we die, I still would not part

I will be their, til time just ends
She will always to me, be more than a friend

OUR BOARDWALK

The sky is clear, & night has fell
Stars are bright, there sounds of shells

The wind is soft, a pleasant breeze
A lake of water, from many seas

Waves in the water, move steadly slow
As the light from the moon, glisten & glows

I'm holding her hand, as we walk on the boardwalk
We're listen to the water, as it howls talks

The wind blowing, giving her a slight chill
She squeezes herself, to give a warm feel

I walked up behind her, and our fingers locked
I gave her a hug, she was shocked

I whispered to her, this feeling is real
The protection & warmth, will be here until

Until I am gone, away forever
But will the love leave, Hmm! Never

Tears started to come, from your eyes
I put my hands in the water, & covered your cries

Shining on us, was the glow from the moon
As the ocean that talked, played a silent toon

I will always be their, to show I care
My love I'll share, her pain I'll spare

The stars in the sky, circled us
I kissed her lips as they sprinkle stardust

The dust made us shine, as we always will
And the years were together, this is how you'll feel
I'm here for you always

MAGIC

One silent night, we wore sitting alone
Sitting on her couch, at her home

I placed her head, on my chest
She looked sleepy, so I thought she should rest

Things got quiet, & oh so still
We both were together, Oh! How this feels

We both fell asleep, into each others dream
Into a fantastic world, of a romantic scene

We found ourselves, on a pillow of clouds
Such happiness & joy, we both look proud

The clouds were moving, gracefully alone
An enchanting place, which nothing go can wrong

Being in the air, with not a care in the world
I held on to her, she was the last ocean pearl

Gliding by a lake, water so calm
I place a little water, inside of my palms

I slung it in the air, there were tiny raindrops
One hit her cheek, I wiped that spot

The clouds lifted us, back into the night
I reached my hand out, to a star that was bright

Now in my hand, the star that's bright
She open my hand, a diamond her sight

The diamond alluring, with her angelic smile
Just like a toy, to a new child

Swosh! A wind came by, & spun us around
Baby! Where did she go, falling to the ground?

She yelled my name, as she fell fast
The yelling stopped, I caught her at last

I looked in her eyes, & told her this
I care for you to much, I could not miss

We've chased for something special, throughout this life
We must hold on it, with all our might

That's when—I woke up, from the dream
And asked me, what does it mean

I looked at her, & went back to sleep
This dream of her, is all I can keep

Should we wake up, or stay in the dream
I don't know, but how I know—how much she means

MY LITTLE ROSE PETAL

Nothing to do, but something on my mind
I take a walk, to past the time

A strong woman, was in my thoughts
My attention & heart, is what she caught

As I walk—a rose, wild but, not tame
Pretty—colorful, it seem to call her name

The petals were red, & some even white
It reminded me of her, it surely would catch your
sight

I took the rose placing petals in my hand
I'm standing at her door, trying to be a man

She open the door, & came on outside

Petals fell, they had a graceful glide

These petals are cute & they are you
So I drop them to your feet, I always think of you

Your eyes were watery, tears ready to fall
I took one petal, & caught them all

This petal will stay, in my heart
Which means you'll be with me, you shall not part

Our eyes were caught, we gaze & stared
We just looked as passion, rose & flared

I palmed your cheek, still in your eyes
I kissed your lips, the emotions flies

Kissing each other, deeply we embrassed
Magic is around, it's been in our face

After the kiss, we held on to each other
No force, No being, could stop these lovers

For the remainder of the night, they stood right there
Letting each other know, they do care

It started with a rose, & ended with a petal
Being with you, I've receive the greatest metal
I really do care

THE RAIN LET OUT & ANGEL

The pain of life, sadness fills the air
No one there, who seem to care

A heart that's cracked, tears falling down
No smile here, just a frown

The point of no return, sorrows & woes
She's balls up inside, the pain it shows

She looked to the Lord, & and ask for rain
To cover her tears & hide her pain

Walking to the back, she stood on the porch
Burning inside, a fiery torch

The fine of sadness that need to be tame
To erase the heartache, tears & pain

She looked to the sky a drop her face
One after another, it seems like a chase

She opened her mouth and started to sing
A soft voice, notes of wings

The weeping of this child, many tears
The rain covered it up, and wash the painful years

The more the rain fell, the harder she sang
Releasing from her heart, the unbearable pain

She sang like and angel, that was first born
Clearer & louder, then a new brass horn

Her pain lifted, & taken away
A message sent, for a coming day

Something coming & something new
To keep her from being, sad & blue

An Angel there, inside her heart
Kept away, like a forgotten art

The rain poured, & it fell

The rain let out & angel

CHRISTMAS MAGIC

Christmas day, the day of the lord
The day that everyone, look towards

A girl was outside, standing on her porch
A wish burning inside, lie a fiery torch

Looking towards the sky, asking for a gift
Her spirit it would rise, her heart it would lift

Appearing from nowhere, standing by the pole
A guy staring at her, in the winter cold

Every step he took, her heart tremble more
Just asking herself, who is he for

From that pole he walked, in front of her eyes
And said, "I'll be here, til the day I die."

Pulling her to him, her head on his chest
It started to snow, she seems to be at rest

He lifted her head, as the emotions did flow
Her eyes, they glisten, as did the snow

Snow on the ground, tiny diamonds all around
Nothing but a smile, not a single frown

He took her hand, they walked in the yard
Swinging her around, being a bodyguard

Those two in the snow, seem to be at another level
No one could take it away, not even the devil

The love that was there, was pure as the snow
So the snow shined, so everyone would know

They kissed again, as their love was fed
As Jesus's star, sparkled over their head

Now they know, what few people see
It's called Christmas Magic, Woman I Love Thee!

A KING AND HIS QUEEN

The day was cold, and gray outside
Being together, hiding inside

Staring at the window, with a gray background
A snowflake fell, not making a sound

Then came more, and fill up the scene
We laid back and began to dream

King and a queen, standing on a cliff
Letting their hair, blow in the drift

Land as far as you can see with your royalty eyes
Some desert, some trees, with a distance disguise

The sun was setting, with a purple outline
They looked over the kingdom, the sun it shined

The two where in love, the type you only feel
Surely in love, their fate was seal

They took off running, playing a chase
Having fun, no time goes to waste

Running across a lake, with a long waterfall
They look at each other, and ran for it all

Swimming to the shore, they laid in a spot
Her paw touch his, their hearts would trot

She look in his eyes, passion unreal
Splashing off the waterfall, their hearts appeal

Making love to the splash, of a starry night
The stars are the witness, of pleasure's delight

Afterward they cuddle, while sitting on a rock
The water was calm, the splash continued, they were
locked

It was the lion king, and she was my queen
A love not forgotten, but rarely ever seen

I'll be your king, until my time

Still be my queen, and in your heart I'll shine
I Love You

CAUSE I LOVE YOU

Not long ago, a boy was alone
With no one to hold, nowhere to belong

A beautiful girl, is all he wanted
So, he could spend, those treasure moments

Now he has the girl, right in his arms
Holding on to her, like an antique charm

He's giving his all, and loving her more
The feelings form his heart, you can hear them pour

Is it love, is it for real?
When their together, it all you can feel

He's placed a rose, as a symbol of his love
A symbol of her, that was given from above

He kissed her lips, like no other
Hoping one day, it may go further

Standing in the aisle, you may kisse the bride
Taking off for a beautiful, & wonderful ride

Now he's sitting, thinking of the past
Trying to make, all the memories last

Giving her hugs, & pulling her close
Imagining their both, on a sandy coast

Picking her up, off her feet
Waiting for their bodies, to connect and meet

Or when she'd in pain, or has a wound
He tends to her need, to heal her soon

Now her child, nothing but joy
He takes it all, and gives her more

Thank you, Lord, for the blooming rose
Of multi-colors, that you have chose

The boy is me, & this is written for you
Why!—Cause I Love You

VOLUME VII

A TROUBLED LAND

In a land that many, have often seen
Few have stayed, some only dream

This land that I speak, is not a myth
The land is love, which is a cliff

Water is smashing, all around
Showing the trouble, hearing harmful sounds

Escaping the trouble, you must face the fear
Scared and timid, you must wipe your tear

Rising off the cliff, is a bridge of love
Which the love you have is what it's made of
With the emotions of love, filled

Now you must cross & surely be brave
Or let the troubles take, the life you gave

The trouble, it sounds, as the bridge you cross
Shaking like a child, feeling so lost

There's a hole in the bridge that you must leap
The love you a wait, is almost at your feet

Why do you fear, is the risk to high?
You look back & see, you just might die

Will you make it, if you seek?
The love is your strength, why don't you see

You jump in the air, but still there's a fright
Will you be caught, or erase from sight?

If the love that's waiting is strong as above
You both will fly away as doves

I'm accepting my fear, because I Love U!
So catch me my love & let's fly into the blue

JUST ONE STAR

How many stars, are in the sky?
Night after night, they soar & fly

I've set in the night, & looked at the stars
Counted each one, I wonder how far

There was one star, out of all the rest
A diamond sparkle, to me it was the best

I've wanted to grab it, so many times
To feel the warmth, from its glowing shine

So, I made a move, to walk toward the sky
Clinching that moment with stars that flies

The trail is long, but I don't care
This is in my heart, I just want to share

Time has passed, sill on the trail
What keeps me there, in the air I'm hailed

Was its lover or desire, or both intertwine
To reach that star, that so brightly shines

Now I know I may never reach this star
But I keep trying & trying, no matter how far

Just a touch or glimpse, of the shined or gleam
That looks so happy, so happy it seems

While on my trail, I keep hearing chimes
Are the other stars, giving me a signs?

This journey I take, to the night skies
Hoping to catch my star that flies

Now there are millions of them, Oh so far
But in my heart, there's, Just One Star!

OUR PLACE IN LOVE

The wind blows, leaves rustle
The tree sway, the branches tussle

A full moon, a ghostly glow
Traces of emotions, feelings flow

A park that's still, but the swings they sway
A waiting for someone, to just come play

Leaning on the tree, was a man
He seems to be clutching, something in his hand

He looks at the park, memories are there
A lady of beauty, her kind is rare

So much was there, so much had passed
Not a memory fade, they all would last

Leaving the tree, he walked toward the swing
He stood behind it, the chains ring

He could see her sitting, as he gave her a push
Even though a memory, he could still hear a swoosh!

A time of fun, & lots of joy
They both were happy, as girl & boy

He strolled back, to the sturdy tree
All the memories there, he truly could see

Looking at his hand, he opens it wide
A peach petal, a star, is what he hides

A gust of wind, came hurdling by
The petal flew behind, it seems to fly

He took the star, & look at the night
Slung it in the air, not a trace of sight

Where is the petal, where did it go?
The petal was the lady, the wind would blow

Surprise was in the air, as she reaches for his hand
They kissed each other, what a happy man

Now the star in the night, lighting the park
An angel in the heavens, playing their harp

There's a place for everyone that means a lot
A place for my love I have not forgot!

I AND MY BROTHER'S SECRET

I and my brother, we stand as young men
Striving to be better, looking for the win

Head up high, standing up proud
Doing what we can, actions will speak loud

We both have chains, to tie us down
We fight with our hearts, they fall to the ground

Fighting with our hearts, to get where we are
Not planning to stop, we will go far

We will be victorious, in everything we do
Looking at our actions, you know it's true

People will look back, why were they so great
And we will say, it must have been fate

Those two young men, they did succeed
They had a secret, that helped them indeed

A beautiful woman, that help us on
Thank you, Grandmother, for being so strong

We love you and always will
So, we have dedicated this to you

Rosa J. Barber

1935–1995

THE GREATEST GIFT
I COULD GIVE

When Jesus was born, he was a gift
Teachings he'd bring, our spirits he'd lift

Well Christmas is here, at this present time
As I stand at my tree, & watch it shine

My tree was enchanting, surrounded with glee
Grasping every moment, that it stands before me

It's time to give, at this time of year
Giving your feelings, letting them appear

Now what do you give, for the one I care
For she is special, my feelings I share

The gift I give, it must be real
Expressing all, emotions I feel

Some men give, diamonds & gold
But without meaning, the story—not told

So, what do I give that means so much
From my heart & soul, she'll be touched

Materials no, it must be more
Showing how, my heart pours

No, their is one gift that I can see
That says it all, & comes from me

I give all I have, & all I am
It's my heart, No sham!

Please accepted my gift, & always treasure
I hope through life, it brings you pleasure

My heart will be here, as we live
Woman, this was the greatest gift I could give!

Merry Christmas

BREAK TIME

Passing time with thoughts, moments that last
Slowly I think, my heart beats fast

Gazing off in time, as I sit in my chair
My face is calm, I am not there

I stare at the lake, that glisten from the sun
The water is captivating, your mind is stun

A bridge & benches, station all around
Towering trees, that make whistling sounds

The season is winter, the breeze is slow
A cool chill, with a steady flow

Some are special, is standing there
Beauty of grace, what could compare

So, I took her hand, as we walk the trail
Silence is our words, love is our spell

Choir swaying trees, play a tune
Clapping ripples, in this lagoon

Making it to the bridge, I stop our motion
Tension & passion, flowing like and ocean

Our eyes met, silence all around
No tree talking, No rippling sound

Passing no words, feeling our thought
Vibrations of love is what we caught

She laid her head, just to rest
Holding her dearly, on my chest

Words are not needed, for moment like these
Knowing the feelings, when your heart is pleased

Break time is over, so now I must go
But a break from you, never so

So I Love You!

ROSE COME BACK HOME

Purple to Orange, Sun setting in the west
Another full day, has come to a rest

The ocean roars, rumbles and thunders
As you ponder and stand, and look and wonder

Pacing the balcony, as I look around
Seeing the beauty, hearing the sounds

I raise to my eyes, a charming red rose
Everything was moving, but I had froze

I twirled the rose, and looked at it sight
My rose was gone, she was my light

Nothing but memories, and a single red rose
I lost a tear, I felt my woe's

I left the affair, to hide my loss
I wish she was here, But I know that's false

Dropping the rose, I went to the reef
The Rose on the balcony, and me underneath

Just as I left, a visitor was there
Walking to the edge, she was so fair

As she walk to the edge, she looked to the floor
The charming red rose, she could not ignore

She lifted the rose, and looked at it's charm
She somehow new, it was protected from harm

Once upon a time, not long ago
A rose petal she was, knows by her Bo

Gazing at the ocean, and the sun going down
Grasping to the memories, that did not drown

She dropped the rose, it fell to my feet
I went upstairs, and who did I see

Actions the same, we never would have known
Calling our memories, and our moments alone

Love is real, and will come back
Still together, and definitely intact

Love hurts, and being alone
My rose came back, she came back home

VOLUME VIII

PRECIOUS ECSTASY

There's a young man walking, down the street
With his head staring, at his feet

Everyone slumbers, this fall midnight
A clear sky, with a starry light

The trees rest, as they are robbed
The winds toon, makes them nod

As leaves are taken, and fall to the ground
You hear his footsteps, cracking sound

Strolling on, with a mellow step
Love in his heart, is what he kept

There's a house, near the pole
Inside is his love, genuine gold

So many words, he wants to say
But so many words, in the way

So many things, He wants to do
So many ways to say, I Love You

Learning on the pole, he feels a vibe
He looks to his left, she standing outside

Beautiful as ever, like the starry nights
A timeless beauty, the finest sight

A conversation, between their eyes
A sweet sensation, of their ties

Saying I Love You, in so many ways
They need to be close, to christen this phase

They walk to each other, but it seem like forever
Running—they made it, clinging together
Hugging & caressing, a breath of relief

Back in their arms, together again
Someone to trust, a valued friend

The strongest love, will test the sea
Conquer the wave, now begins "Precious Ecstasy"

MY END IS MY BEGINNING

Life,
Few things have a till, to survive on & on
Past the limit expected.

Born to end but the end is the beginning
To a survival few have seen.

Place on a dusty rock road, to take that journey
Pos, Holes, crooks, dust lie before.

Parading with heart, unbelievable strength
Blood & tears to the bitter end.

Falling to your knees from devastating pain
Rise to your feet with strength from God.

Continue with your heart to complete the end

Reach, Reach, Reach! For the line

Riches awaiting, rewards been there
You have to travel the road appreciate the reward.